Also by Alan j. Wright

Media Starters
Cosmo's Cure
Quality Conversations in the Classroom
Reading Comprehension—Alan Wright et al.
Igniting Writing: When a Teacher Writes
Searching for Hen's Teeth: Poetry
from the Search Zone
I Bet There's No Broccoli on the Moon:
More poetry from the Search Zone

WHAT THE
POEMSTER
FOUND

Poems from Places Poets Roam

ALAN j WRIGHT

BALBOA.
PRESS

A DIVISION OF HAY HOUSE

Balboa Press books may be ordered through booksellers or by contacting:

Balboa Press
A Division of Hay House
1663 Liberty Drive
Bloomington, IN 47403
www.balboapress.com.au
1 (877) 407-4847

Print information available on the last page.

ISBN: 978-1-5043-1952-2 (sc)
ISBN: 978-1-5043-1953-9 (e)

Balboa Press rev. date: 10/30/2019

During the six years I lived in New York City, I often visited a café on 57th Street. In that busy little café, they sold a hearty winter soup. The café proudly displayed a sign announcing 'ten vegetable soup.' It was mighty impressive soup, I must say. Warm, chunky and wholesome. It warmed me against the New York winter, many a time.

Well, this anthology of poems is a bit like that soup. It has been made using lots of ingredients. It contains a mix of poetic styles and the poems deal with a broad range of subjects.

On the pages ahead, lie poems written to amuse. Others celebrate nonsense. I love a bit of nonsense in my life. It stops the serious world from taking over.

At the other end of the scale, I have chosen poems dealing with a range of issues, because poets 'make' their poems for different reasons. Sometimes a poet wants to make a statement or draw attention to something they want the world to know about, think about, or notice.

You will discover poems about past events, while others try to capture small moments in my life. Moments I consider worthy of preserving and sharing.

The title of this book, 'What the Poemster Found' owes it origins to a boy I met in a school I was visiting. He looked at me and asked, 'Are you the Poemster?' So, sitting in the soft shadows of a winter afternoon I suddenly had my title. It can be like that sometimes. You just get lucky...

Poets constantly scan their lives for writing ideas. We must remain ever ready to capture them when they come floating by. All writers must learn to become close observers of their world.

It is often said the best books to read are those that challenge us to think. I hope the poems in this book provide you with some laughter and smiles, but I also hope they give you something to ponder as well. Enjoy the poetry soup.

Alan j Wright

No poems were injured in the making of this book

For Frank Harris, my Grade 6 teacher at Monbulk Primary School, who awakened my poet's heart.

Contents

Opposite Positions

I think the opposite of skinny
Is the bottom on my Auntie Minnie
What is the opposite of dark?
A flashlight beam- bold and stark
What is the opposite of fit?
Someone who prefers to sit
The opposite of sweet, I think
Are my brother's shoes-they really stink
The opposite of underwear
Are the clothes on top, we wear out there
The very opposite of happy
Is someone cranky, nasty, snappy
It's screaming, yelling, don't come near
It's go away, don't want you here
The very opposite of morning
Is late at night when I start yawning
It's darkness falling around
When nightfall covers all the ground
And if purple has an opposite
I'm certain I can't think of it

The Words That Come At Night

Sometimes
The words of unwritten poems
Slide into bed next to me
They nestle on my pillow
And whisper in my ear
Write me down
Write me down
-Remember me
In tomorrow's early light

Soft echoes at the edge of sleep
Implore me to
Commit to memory
Sweet refrains and edgy fragments
These faint murmurings
These wannabe words of unwritten poems
Settle as cobweb fine
Final thoughts
Last visitors
Before sleep swallows the room

Pen Licence Perils

Yesterday
Tomorrow looked so much better
Than it does today...
Doubt is now all around me
It rumbles like thunder in the distance
Personally, I think pen licences are a bit silly
But, my teacher thinks we must have one before we can
Give up our pencils
I just want to write
-sometimes with a pen
-sometimes with a pencil
I don't need a book licence to read
So, why do I need a pen licence?
Today, I grip my pencil more tightly
Words form reluctantly on the page
Nervous letters
Shaky *S'-es*
Trembling *T's*
Yesterday
Tomorrow looked so much better
Than it does today
I never needed a knife and fork licence
Or a shoelace tying licence
Pen licences should be struck off
With the stroke of a...
Of -a pen

The Sad and Untimely Death of Brutus the Budgerigar

Kenny Middleton
-a kid in my class
Came to school yesterday and announced to the whole
class during Show and Tell
My Mum is a killer!
Just blurted it out to the whole class
Miss Warren, our teacher
Almost fainted with shock
'Whatever do you mean young man?'
'Well,' said Kenny Middleton
'Mum killed Brutus our pet budgerigar this morning.
She said it was purely an accident
-and it was
But she killed him just the same.'

Miss Warren was in total shock
The whole class stared in amazement
Kenny's comments had rocked the room
'What's a budgerigar? Asked Anastasia
'Let me explain' Kenny said
'Yes please' everyone chimed in…

'We were about to leave for school when
Mum gets a brainwave
-Decides she will quickly vacuum the carpet
before we all pile into the car
That's Mum, three kids and our dog, Mungo
So she fires up the vacuum
Brooomm, Whooo!

The vacuum Mum calls the Dust Devil whirrs to life
Back and forth across the carpet
Mum pushes and pulls the Dust Devil
-she's almost finished
When something catches her eye.

Brutus the budgie
Hates loud noises
The Dust Devil makes him very nervous
So he chirps and cheeps and flaps his feather about in his cage
When the vacuum bedevils him
But Mum doesn't see Brutus
She doesn't see his distress
Oh no
Mum only sees the seeds and the mess on the floor of his cage

And that's when she has a huge brain fade...
She sticks the nozzle of the whirring vacuum into the cage
And its supersonic suction sucks up seeds and mess
Everything!
-including poor little Brutus!
He's gone in a flash of feathers
Devoured by the Dust Devil
Faarr-loop!
Mum Screamed
We all screamed
But it was a bit too late for Brutus
He'd gone to Budgerigar heaven.'

A tear appeared in Kenny's eye
His Mum keeps apologizing, he says
But it won't bring Brutus back…

Kenny told us he now wants an eagle as a pet
Or, maybe an emu
-Anything that can't be swallowed by a Dust Devil

Visitations

On Monday
Drove to Chinkapook
Stopped a while
To take a look
On Tuesday,
Zipped to Geelong
Scanned the harbour
-But didn't stay long.
On Wednesday,
Travelled to Boggabri
Bought some cheese
-Not sure why.
On Thursday,
Drove through Yackandandah
Flowers were blooming
So I took a gander.
On Friday,
Arrived in Mollymook
Found a shop,
Bought a book.
On Saturday
Was in Woolloomooloo
Couldn't believe it
-so were you!
On Sunday
I stayed home.
-Didn't travel
-Didn't roam.

Wheel Bad News

we all know
the wheels on the bus
go round and round,
round and round.

so, why is it
that the wheels on the
shopping trolley
go wibble-wobble, wonk
wibble-wobble, wonk?

they should be going
round and round,
round and round
-just like the wheels on the bus
go round and round.

it's wheely bad, I tell you
-wheely bad.

I'm Not Here

I'm sitting under the shade of a Peppercorn tree
In the playground
I'm munching on a juicy apple when Martin Fluendi
-a kid two grades below me
Wanders by
Sits down
And just stares at my apple
It's all a bit strange if you ask me

So, I say
Hey Martin, I can prove I'm not here
Huh?
Well, am I in Sydney?
No
Am I in Adelaide?
No
Well, if I'm not in Sydney or Adelaide
I must be somewhere else, true?
True
Well, if I'm somewhere else, I can't be here, can I?
Huh?

Martin stands up and wanders off across the playground
Looks back at me
One more time
While scratching his head
I look at my half eaten juicy apple and smile
CRUNCH!

Look At Me, Look at Me

You've seen them I'm sure
With their selfie sticks
Their lofted totems
Click, click, click

Snap, snap, snap
What do you see?
In my selfie library?
It's just 400 snaps of me, me, me

-Look at me, looking at me
Kissy face, kissy face
Flout the pout
Flout the pout
Push those luscious lips
Right out
Jump, pose
Leap in the air
Take a shot of me, somewhere

Get my best side
Get it quick
Get it quickly, that's the trick
Gather round, all lean in
Magnet heads
Smile, grin

This is me at the Eiffel Tower
Get an eyeful of me
The tower's there too –somewhere

This is me at the Opera House
-My hair looks great, I was feeling grouse
This is me at the Taj- whatever
It's a gorgeous shot of me and Trevor

Wherever they go
It's the same selection
It has to be their own reflection
-Again and again and again

This self-obsession
This new sensation
Just like Narcissus
It's a pre-occupation

Aloft they hold that selfie stick
Another snap
Another click
Such adoration,
What is it they see?
Just themselves -unfortunately

The Ride of the Sky Witch

Upon her broom a witch goes riding.
Cloaked in darkness,
Dipping, gliding.

Away she sweeps across the sky.
All cackle and howl,
And mournful cry.

In the gathering evening gloom.
She hovers in shadows,
And swoops with her broom

Spells are muttered to the darkened sky
And then with a whoop
Away she will fly

Along the laneway, through the street
Her evening ride
Is short and sweet

A final swoop above the town
Then homeward bound
Her broom heads down

Compound Interest

You are the jingle in my bells
The tick in my tock
The flash in my light
The spring in my time
The whirl in my wind
The tell in my tale
You are the ever in my lasting
The ginger in my bread
The life in my boat
It has to be said

Hanoi Morning

The sky
Seamless,
Heavy,
Drapes itself suffocatingly
Over a muggy Hanoi street scene
The thunder gods
Argue endlessly.
Clamorous behind a curtain of gun metal grey cloud.

These daily squabbles frequently end in tears.
The people are not dismayed.
Plastic ponchos and umbrellas
Emerge with the suddenness
of rabbits from a magician's hat

Such is the way of the wet season.

In This Place

In this place
Words swarm and sing in my head
And I experience a splendid isolation
Coffee aromas swirl and drift in the air
The various conversations of café customers
Nip at the silence
Today the music plays on
Unremarkable and unrecognised
Like the last kids picked for the team
In this place
I arm myself
With pen and paper
And loosen my mind with my cappuccino companion
I shall harness my tumbling thoughts
And be a writer in a wild world
Revealing mysteries
Revelling in the moment
Of inspirational magic
A word collector
A page coverer
Separate from the hubbub
Around me

Chilly Winds Out There

Winter grins
Chilly winds
Teeth are all a chatter
Rug up tight
Fading light
Falling leaves all scatter.

Winter grins
Chilly winds
Icy gales blow
Step around
Muddy ground
Everywhere I go.

Winter grins
Chilly winds
Clouds gather in a cluster
Lightning flashes
Thunder crashes
Tis a menacing southerly buster.

Winter grins
Chilly winds
Race to beat the storm
Shut the door
Against the roar,
Inside, safe and warm.

The Sad Tale of Norman Neets

Norman Neets would eat sugary sweets
Chocolate,
Lollies,
Ice-cream.

He refused to eat beans
Tomatoes
Or greens
And pumpkin made Norm
Throw a fit

With a diet so weird
It was just as we feared
And Norman
Underwent changes

His face turned pale
He sprouted a tale
His arms and his legs
Became rather frail

His hair became ropey
He appeared somewhat dopey
And at night
Norman howled at the moon

So children, let Norm be a lesson
Please, eat up all your greens
If you refuse,
You're igniting a fuse
With outcomes quite unforeseen.

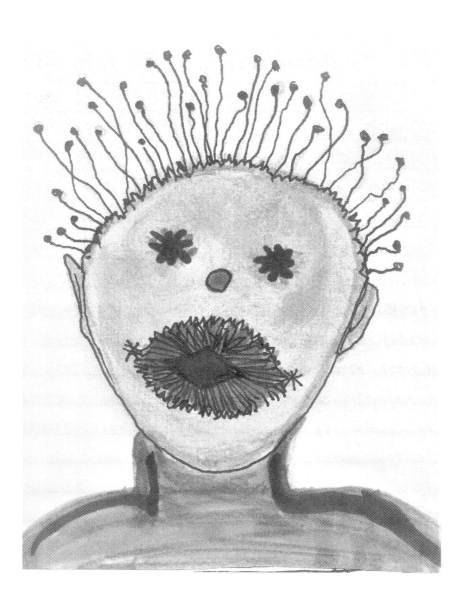

Time to Skedaddle

Don't be a dingbat
I'll be back,
Lickety split
Just like that
All hurry-scurry
Ooh la-la
Don't shilly-shally
It won't get you far
Holy-moly
Okey-doke
Watch me vanish
In a puff of smoke
No time for ratbags
Protect your wicket
Stay alert
That's the ticket!

The Moon and Me

The moon seems bright
In the sky tonight.
It glows like a child's smile.
I witnessed its great majesty close to midnight
When I took my dog out for her end of evening snuffle
and wander.

In all honesty,
I should have lingered longer.
-And paid the moon its due attention.
But for me and the moon,
It is an enduring relationship of fleeting admiration.

It's always been like that
For the moon and me.

Consider This

Do you dream of mystic places?
Do you dream of mighty deeds?
Do you travel in your mind?
As you stand among the weeds?

Do you stare at the horizon?
Do you step up to the plate?
Do you seek out new adventures?
Or have you simply locked the gate?

Live Stupid, Die Dumb

I hold no desire
To live stupid
To die dumb.
I choose to move in the opposite direction to those feckless folk
Who cling to ignorance like a bulldog with a bone
Stupid is easy
You can get there in a flash.
Just put up the vacant sign in your brain.
Let weeds flourish around your thoughts.
Pull up the drawbridge on fresh ideas.
Just turn away.
Turn away from reading
Consider it unnecessary
Banish books from your life
Let them gather dust
-Just as your mind will surely gather dust.
Never ask questions,
Refuse to listen,
Refuse to try,
Pack up your dreams,
Lock them away in a cupboard
And forget about them.
Cover your ears to new ideas,
Plant yourself in the dark.
Never leave.
Ignore the world out there.
Never travel beyond the city limits.
Never lose sight of the shore, what's more,
Embrace your shackles
Avoid taking risks

Dangerous thing, risk.
Yes, stupid is yours for the taking
Giving up is easy, so easy.
But remember...
Remember, if you can
To live stupid
To die dumb
Is a dead, set, choice!

Poembrew

A poem is brewing in my brain.
In the far reaches of thought and contemplation
Words assemble in ones and twos
Clusters and battalions.
Sweet lines with potent phrasing
Float on the horizon of possibility
Inviting attention.
A poem is brewing in my brain
Words clang, collide and collude
Jostling for best position.
A song of composition
Rises gradually across days and nights
Bringing with it rhyme and reason
As the focus sharpens.
A poem is brewing in my brain
It pops and sparks and sizzles.
I wait patiently for its arrival
As one would a visit from a friend.
A poem is brewing in my brain.
Soon it will spill across the pages of my notebook.
Words shaped and massaged to fit their allotted spaces.
Words warm and raw
Some slide easily onto the line.
Others snap into place
Like Lego pieces,
As they take up position
In readiness for the poet's pop-eyed approval.

Slugger-Mugger

The Slugger-Mugger's coming
Slugger-Mugger
Slugger-Mugger
The Slugger- Mugger's coming
Sliding in on slime

The Slugger- Mugger's coming
The conditions are just right
The moon is hidden by the clouds
There's very little light

The Slugger- Mugger's on the way
To your neighbourhood
Please don't bother hiding
It won't do you any good

The slugger- Mugger's searching
For kids who don't eat greens
They leave them on the plate
They hide them in their jeans

Spinach, peas and broccoli
Parsley, lettuce and beans
Shunned by fussy eaters
-such distressing scenes
The Slugger- Mugger will find them
It's only a matter of time
The Slugger-Mugger's ready
To splatter them in slime

Sticky-icky green slime
And Slugger-Mugger spit
It takes days to remove it
You need a cleaning kit

The Slugger-Mugger's coming
Consider this a warning
If you don't eat your greens
You might look slimy in the morning

The Slugger-Mugger's coming
Sliding in on slime
If you refuse to eat your greens
You are running out of time

Slugger- Mugger...

Two 12 Word Poems

Birdsong

In the morning
Magpies carol
Joyfully
This
Daily birdsong
Warms my heart

Cruel Wind

The cruel wind
Complains noisily
Whoosh
Push
Howling, screaming
Blow hard, bully

Big Dry

I stand under the eaves
Seeking salvation from the unrelenting sun.
Disturbed by the hot wind
Leaves with hues like dry straw, swirl at my feet
A faint fizmer is whispered as they dervish and dance
Scraunching and brittle.
Dust scatters in puffs
Rising
Before gently settling
On every available surface.

An eagle hovers,
Between the baked-earth land
With the blazing sun
Supreme against the cloudless sky.

Far off,
The horizon dances the shimmer
While an old brown dog
Lazes inside the shadow line beside the house.

Moisture is a stranger
In this bone dry world.
No dewdrops reside here.
The dry season
Parches everything,
Everyone.
This pitiless season
Sheds no tears.

Lawn Thoughts

Mowing the lawn
Is clippings in your hair
Up your nose
In your socks
Mowing the lawn
Is smoky fumes
Swishing blades
Aromas of cut grass
Mowing the lawn
Is hugging the edges
Avoiding the cat
Gliding past Mum's chrysanthemums
Mowing the lawn
Is refilling the tank
Dumping the clippings
Raking and sweeping
Mowing the lawn
A neat, grassy haircut
A summer chore

-And pocket money

Springtime Revelations

Finessing all the shrubbery,
the gentle breeze washed over me.
Scents and bouquets then arose.
The earth reveals what winter knows.

The morning air is light and warm.
Dragonflies hover, bees do swarm.
The season's proudest blooms it shows.
The earth reveals what winter knows.

The garden's leafy vestments swell.
Winter's over, all is well.
The daffodils emerge in rows.
The earth reveals what winter knows.

A time of great fecundity,
and colours worn so blushingly.
Fruitfulness in springtime grows.
The earth reveals what winter knows.

Summer Comes Rushing

Summer comes rushing towards me
Wearing sneakers
Smiling
And smelling of sunscreen and salt water
It dances on the shoreline
Barefoot, joyful
While licking an ice-cream
And humming, *The Boys of Summer*
It carries under its arm
Sunsets the colour of ripened
Nectarines

Cicadas sing as it glides by
And the saphirine sea
Sparkles

Summertime
Shimmer time
Summer shine

The Life of Leon

He's a tough guy, Leon
Attitude locked
Fire in his eyes
It's all hard knocks
Leon's a cracker
Eyebrow scarred
Dynamite hands
A heart so hard
On the street
Where dangers lurk
Another kid
Whose dreams don't work
Here comes Leon
Better scurry
Bamma-lamma
In a hurry
Angry kid
Unwashed hair
Look away
From his mad dog stare
Out of home
On the street
Never quite sure
What he's got to eat

Struts about
With the craggy crew
Cigarettes
High top shoes
Leon's coming
Rats all scurry
Bamma–lamma
Better hurry
Slaps away
Any helping hand
Zero trust
Anger fanned
He's got swagger
He's got sneer
Built a wall around
Inner fears
Violent father
Junkie Mum
Winter nights
Sleep won't come
There goes Leon
Twelve years old
Bamma-lamma
Fortune's sold

A Massive Murder of Crows

I went walking under a seamless grey sky
In search of a sandwich shop
I ambled past a giant tree
Deciduous
Its naked winter branches
Adorned with a massive murder of crows
A raucous chorus of calamitous cawing
Scraped the sky
Crow feathers all soot and cinders
Like black leaves

Crows perched starkly in a winter tree
Contrasting the grey curtain of the sky

A massive murder of crows
And a sense of misgiving
Cawing
Cawing
Pathetic jagged notes rising up
On a black day in July

A Degree of Uncertainty

The magpie knows
When it is safe to swoop from the high branch of the
Eucalypt
And alight upon the ground
The leaf knows when
It is time to let go
The wave breaks when it is ready
And the breeze wafts where it wishes
I sit
Fastened to my chair
Pondering my next move

So Sorry

Forgive me dear daddy
I know I've done wrong
But your face might stay twisted
If you're angry too long
Smile at me mummy
Make life worth living
I'll be an angel
If you'll be forgiving

Please Sir

Please Sir
Colin Raggleston
Keeps staring at me
He stares at me with his gigantic fishy eyes
He smiles at me with his crooked smile
And his missing front teeth
He does weird things with his eyebrows
His eyes roll round and round
They cross over
He makes them disappear
He pretends to take them out
And he thinks that is so funny
So funny -but, it isn't
He stares at me
When I'm eating my lunch
Yesterday, he dribbled yoghurt down his chin
He sends me notes saying things like
C R 4 U
He walks home from school
The same way I do
Even though he lives four blocks away
In the opposite direction
And during art lessons
He tries to lend me pencils he says he has kissed
-Yesterday
During playtime
He tried to offer me a bite of his half eaten apple
Please Sir
Make him stop

My Other Hat

My other hat

Is large and red
It covers my ears
It must be said
It covers my eyes
It covers my feet
There's room at the back
For a small wooden seat

It's fair to say my hat's immense
The brim is enclosed
By a high metal fence
With a viewing platform at the peak
This hat of mine
Is truly unique.

The Old Jalopy

Dad looks stressed
Mum looks stroppy
We're going for a drive
In our old jalopy
Kids pile in
Dogs in tow
Shut the doors
And we're set to go
Turn the key
Pull the choke
There's a great loud bang
And a tiny puff of smoke
Four false starts
Before the engine splutters
Whoops and hollers
Heart's aflutter
Shake and rattle
Lurch and cough
And finally the car takes off!
Down the road
Into town
The wildest ride
For miles around
Dad starts singing
Mum's not stroppy
Oh what fun!
-In our old jalopy

Images of A Grandfather Clock

The Grandfather clock
Stood tall like a palace guard
Marking time in Nana's lounge-room
Against the wall
Avoiding the sunlight streaming through lace curtained windows
Tick-tocking as the pendulum swung in its unerring arc
Brass and chains and moving arms
Encased behind a long glass face
The clock announced the passing of each hour
With blare and boom
The rowdy ringing out
Chased the silence from the room
Why so loud? the small ones asked
Why so tall? the small ones wondered
They kept their distance
Time moved on relentlessly
The Grandfather clock
Stood tall like a palace guard
Marking time in Nana's lounge-room

wants and Needs

Danny wants an X Box
Shani wants a bike
Kelly wants some high top sneakers that constantly
glow in the dark
Khalil wants his mother to stop crying

Michelle wants a holiday in a tropical resort
Charlie wants new soccer boots –bright, shiny red
Olivia wants a new laptop computer
Khalil wants the bombs to stop falling on his town

Mandy wants a basketball
Joel a new CD
Max wants a motorbike and a new wetsuit
Khalil wants to spend a night without wailing sirens

Swarm

A swarm of locusts
Black out the sun
Turning day into night
Launching themselves
With spectacular flight
The beating of a billion wings
Creates a thunderous roar

Every plant
Every blade of grass
Every leaf
Every tiny bush
Is devoured
As the swarm feasts on the helpless landscape

They leave behind
Not a skerrick
They leave behind
No morsel of food
They leave behind-
Starvation
Misery
They remove hope.

Football Dreams in Autumn

He leaps towards the clouds above an imaginary pack
of players
Flying high like all his footballing heroes
In his high top Jenkin boots.
A little dreamer,
Treading the hard turf of another pre-season
He will soon join the March champions and the half
time heroes
But only when the growing and the knowing is done

He spends those autumn mornings
Kicking the dew from the grass
Gripping the Sherrin with deliberate intent
Perfecting the ball drop
Torpedo and drop punt
Controlling the bounce
Peppering the goals from every possible angle
Drop, snap and hope
Step back and line up the shot on goal
This kick
This shot for goal could win the game
Everything hangs on his kick
Nothing less than a goal will do…

These day are made for dreaming
Running with the ball.
All alone on a country footy ground,
Ringed by a fence
Of white wooden pickets

A tufted grassy space
Complete with a lonely scoreboard
Paint peeling forlorn
And gnarly goalposts keeping up the ends
Just the magpies in nearby gumtrees for company
Feathered spectators
An oval with a visibly imperfect slope.
-His field for dreaming.
He stands in the goal-square
At the ground's highest point
And kicks the ball with all his might
Again and again.
-And yet again
The day will come when he can launch that ball
Barrelling its way to the ground's centre
-But not yet

All this on his field for dreaming
On these autumn mornings
Kicking the dew from the grass
A boy
A little dreamer
A football
And a couple of hours of kick and fetch
Again and again
All alone on a country footy ground

where Does My poetry Hide?

Where does my poetry hide?
It snuggles in snatches of conversations
floating down the street
It rocks about in my collected treasures
Junky and jumbled

I look for it in lettuce, limes and lemons
In asparagus, apples, even anchovies
It might be sealed a packet of peppermints
A jar of peanut butter
Escaping with aromatic intensity
Poetry washes up on the shoreline
in clusters of seashells
Glittering sea glass
Seaweed and wet sand

I seek it out in a song's refrain
And voices in a playground
I find it nestling in my favourite books
It emerges in isolated words
-and fabulous fragments
Angry and otherwise
It swirls in the mumbles and whispers rumbling
against the internal walls of houses.
It develops in photographs that magically reveal my
history

Poetry soothes me in sonorous voices on the radio
And thunders at me on stormy mornings
I can spot it in a day old newspaper article
Or a marescent autumn leaf

Poetry reveals itself in a small child's eyes
It announces itself in simple pleasures,
Or recollections of days long past
It is minute like smidgens and skerricks
Things barely seen or blown to smithereens
It is immense like boulders, bridges and reservoirs

I hear poetry in the morning carols of magpies
I wake each day knowing it's out there
waiting for me to discover its hiding spots
-Coming, ready or not.

Who's at the Door?

I heard a knocking at my door
With urgency it did implore
Investigation was required
My curiosity was duly fired
I opened up
And I espied
The wind
Insisting it should come inside

Feather

Filmy plumage
Ever wispy
Against the skin, a light and downy touch
The tufted and the smooth
Have the vultures been short changed?
Every hat benefits from the addition of a few
Ruffled or royal and worn like shimmering jewels

The Manifesto of Alvin j Riot

Be prepared to explore the outer limits of your own
potential
Discard your socks if your toe pokes through
Always wear comfortable underwear
Go fishing just to be alone with your thoughts
Chip away at your ignorance -read
If you catch a fish consider it an added bonus
If the sign says fast food think about it slowly
Never meditate in the middle of the road
Embrace simple pleasures
Take time to listen to music every day
Stop feeling guilty if your favourite ice cream flavour
is vanilla
Hold hands
Wherever you are- be there!
Try to find a job that brings you satisfaction
Challenge the claim that New York is the capital of
the world
Make certain the person you marry is your best friend
Avoid conservatives. They are the beige people.
Don't throw bricks straight up
Sleep in a comfortable bed
Appreciate your pillow
Sand between your toes is okay. Sand in your shorts
isn't
Never wear tight clothes on a long trip
Put things back the way you found them- except
large maps
Don't be afraid to pick up litter
Never take the words I love you for granted
Remember it's just one big ocean- keep it clean

Don't feel guilty about disliking cats
Go to Venice at least once in your life
Buy a vanilla slice and savour the flavour
Never beg, never steal
It's okay to borrow toilet paper though
Every stop is a place to start
Always take your socks off before you get into bed
Drive until you come to a T intersection if that's what
you want to do
Never forget that sheep are stupid
Laugh at yourself
Don't worry if you get tongue tied trying to
pronounce, Namibia
Play hide and seek in the supermarket occasionally
Be pedantic if you feel like it
Walk away from boring people
Listen to birdsong in the morning
Lie on the grass and watch the clouds float past –but
not during a thunderstorm!
Don't dare someone to slap you in the face with a wet
fish
Skip down the street if the mood takes you.
Resist television evangelists for God's sake!
Rail against the dimming of the light
Enjoy every season
Seek out sunsets and sunrises
Once you've seen one shopping centre, you've seen a
mall.
Anyone can be a poet
Me, you- the man who nicked my favourite coat,
anyone.

Doughnut Dilemma

There's a hole in my doughnut
Dear Henry, dear Henry
There's a hole in my doughnut
Dear Henry
-a hole
It's meant to be there
Dear Liza, dear Liza
It's meant to be there
Dear Liza
So there!
How shall I fix it?
Dear Henry, dear Henry
How shall I fix it?
Dear Henry
Pray tell
Just eat it
Dear Liza, dear Liza
Just eat it
Dear Liza
And I'll get some peace.

Pigs Might Fly

Birds fly, so might I
Said the pig...
My word, said the bird
No drama, said the llama
Might take a while, said the crocodile
Up there? Asked the bear
Is that legal? Asked the eagle
Dream on, said the swan
Good luck, said the duck
Oh no, said the crow
You won't get far, said the galah
Better me than you, said the emu
I'm heading for cover, said the plover
It's hard not to laugh, said the giraffe

Can I come too? Asked the kangaroo

What's In A Name?

My name was once Red Dog
-running wild and free
A footballing fanatic
My real name is Logophile
-the one who loves words

Today my name is Arnie, the Prickly Bear
Tomorrow, my name will be Story Saver
In dreams, my name isn't Roy Orbison,
It is Light Seeker

Next week, my name will be Buster Smith
The week after, Alvin Riot

Sometimes, my name is Earnest One, Al Pal or Frivolous
Dancer
I'd rather be called, Rupert than Stupid

Secretly, I know my name is Curious Wanderer
You, may call me Lefty
You, (and Paul Simon) may call me Al

Perfect Beach Day

Adventure and discoveries
Await the curious child
Exploring the sweeping line of the beach

Meandering through the shallows
With seagulls for company

The breeze creates kiss curls on waves
Before they rendezvous
with the shoreline

-A chorus of ripples and slaps
The soundtrack of the sea
Back-grounds the scene

Sunset draws a russet curtain across a beach day
A day- close to perfection.

Opportunity Knocks

Chances are given
Opportunities present
Grasp them
Grab them
Before they up and disappear
Before they get swallowed up
By hungrier
Braver souls
Don't miss out
Don't be disappointed
Don't become a sorrowful sad sack

Today
Right now
Step up
Be a brave Dave
A risk taking Rhonda

Embrace every opportchancity!

My Dad was a Rain-man

I stood beside my dad one summer afternoon
Under the eaves of the back veranda
As indigo clouds
Blotted out the summer sky
And threw our world into warm shadows
Dad broke the silence
Can you smell the rain?
-It's only minutes away

So we waited
Staring skyward
Listening to low rumbling of distant thunder
As lightning scratched the sky
And the clouds sprung leaks
Soon large, heavy droplets
Slapped the ground
Before a downpour drenched the day
Stripping dust from the air around us
Making everything fireproof

He knew rain my Dad
He could read the sky
I saw him do it once

Hard Lines

I stand in line
A line stretching forever
A line for which I have no time
A line for which I have no mind
Not even a line in the sand
Not the line of least resistance
Not a fine line
A line that moves with no urgency
A line so lacking in movement
-A snail would grow impatient
I stand in line
The summer sun bites my back
I'm on the hotline
The firing line
And the smallest shuffle excites me
A line longer than a thousand snakes
Stretching out of sight
Beyond the blue horizon
A line capable of joining day to night
A line so long, I want to say-so long
And as I stand in this endless line
-A thought, most disturbing comes rushing at me...
Will there be any ice-creams left
When, finally I reach the head of the queue?
That's the bottom line.

Room for Improvement

Young Sam McCoy is full of gloom
His Mum has just condemned his room
She couldn't stand it anymore
So hung a sign outside his door
She had warned
Begged and pleaded
A giant clean-up is what's needed
I tell you Sam, his mother said
There's no room for a foot to tread

In the corner stands your fish tank
With its growth of weedy slime
Something lives in there, I know
-I saw it move one time
I can smell the old school lunches
Which you bring home and then lose
And that mouldy strong aroma
-Are they hiding in your shoes?

Jeans hang from the curtains
Shirts lie on the floor
The carpet feels quite crunchy
There's a lizard in your drawer
Your teddy bear has lost his head
Your train set doesn't run
I found bacon on your pillow
Along with toothpaste and a bun
I'm not game to open cupboards
For fear of falling rocks
The vacuum jammed this morning

In a pile of stinky socks
Your love of all things putrid
Is over I'm afraid
The clean-up starts this instant
-And she handed Sam a spade

wishing well

I wish my socks didn't grow holes
Darn socks!
I wish I could say synthesizer without biting my tongue
I wish I didn't blush when Margo comes near me
I wish shoes didn't break
And that I had a spare safety pin when I needed one
-or two
I wish runny noses didn't
-Run
I wish cat food didn't smell so incredibly bad
I wish I wasn't afraid of heights
-I'm okay with widths though
I wish I had more time when time is running out
I wish empty milk bottles weren't left in the fridge for
me to find
And that soup refused to spill on my favourite shirt
I wish you a happy birthday
I wish my wishes came true
Except the one about Ronny Wunders
--because we're friends again
And I don't want him to wake up in his underwear
In the shopping centre on a Saturday morning

Port Lincoln Time

I'm in Port Lincoln
Sittin'
Thinkin'
Lookin' across Boston Bay
Starin'
Blinkin'
The sun through the pines is a winkin'
I have a coffee
I'm slowly
Drinkin'
Still thinkin'
In Port Lincoln

The Voyage of Pierre La Plodd

A young man
Pierre La Plodd
Did something that was brave
-Yet odd
He sailed from Calais
To the Bahamas
Wearing only red pyjamas
The kind folk of the Caribbean
Could not believe what they were seein'

Adorned in red, aboard a boat
Relieved that he was still afloat
The Frenchman gained their wild applause
Congratulations, cheers and roars
Pierre stood by all dressed in red
And then announced, it's time for bed.

A Pen for My Thoughts

My black gel pen glides
Across the open white page
Of my word hungry notebook
Words spread out on paper
Words sharply contrasting
This white, lined backdrop
Like a housefly
Landing in a bowl of rice
Words on white paper
Ready to stir
A reader's thought
Gently
As a spoon treats a cup of tea.

No Rhyme This Time Occasion

I'm trying to stop this poem
From rhyming
But I find my anxiety is steadily ~~climbing~~ increasing
Words keep forming in my mind
You know the ones
The usual rhyming ~~kind~~ sort
A childhood filled with rhyming verse
Just makes the situation ~~worse~~ poorer
I'll stay alert
So those rhymes do not intrude
I'll find other words
With which to ~~conclude~~ end
Don't get me wrong
Rhyme is okay
I just want this poem to form
In a whole different ~~way~~ manner

Around The Kitchen Table

This table listens to our secret conversations
Yet reveals nothing
It watches babies grow
Eavesdrops on discussions
-Marvellous
-Mundane
Heartbreaking and ridiculous
This table witnesses the emergence of wisdom
Through the years
Through the march of time
to and fro across its ever flat surface
Words weave and wander
-Sting
-Delight
Comfort and stir
This table silently acquires
Cuts and scrapes
And the accidental spills and splashes
from the merriment of meals and moments shared
This table
Anchors our shared existence
Keeps us together
Provides a meeting place
Yet reveals nothing.

Memories of Yesterdays

Sometimes memories of my yesterdays
Get mixed up inside my head
All I miss tumbles around like clothes in a dryer

Whispers of long gone days float back
Scents and sounds wrap around recollections of then
Seeking attention
Like constantly jumping children

I hear my mother singing as she irons the sheets
The smell of fresh washing rising from the laundry
basket beside her
My father whistles as sweat forms on his brow
As he bends to the rhythm of sawing wood
- creating sawdust

For a flicker in time
They return to now

Sometimes the memories of my yesterdays
And whispers of long gone days
Float back...

Beating the Blank Page
A Battle-Cry for the Brave Young Writer

Hello blank page
I'm here to let you know
You hold no fear for me
I come prepared
For above all things, I am a mighty writer
A writer armed with fearless words
And clever, tenacious ideas
Your unmarked surface
Your dazzling, papery blankness
Are no match for a word warrior
Such as me
I shall stare you down
I shall annoy you
I shall employ you
I shall destroy you, one word at a time
Watch as the irresistible spread of my words take over
My powerful phrases
My vivid verbs
My agile adjectives
Letter by letter
Bit by bit
Your landscape will be transformed
Your emptiness filled

You hold no fear for me, Blanky-Blank Page
For I remain forever and always- a mighty writer
And I shall stare you down
-Take my word for it.

Joan's Toes

We had dancing lessons
In high school
In preparation for the prom
My regular dance partner
Was a sweet, amiable girl
-Joan Hammond

Joan's toes were the sad victims
Of my faltering feet
My stumbling steps
My weedy waltzing

Joan's toes
Innocent casualties
Of my feral foxtrot
My ponderous prancing
It was kind to call it dancing

Slightly Different Dennis

Saw your name in the papers
Watched you on the news
You've become quite famous
For your outlandish views

You always showed a talent
Even when in school
For attracting some attention
When behaving like a fool

Now you stand up on your soapbox
And scream out at the sky
With tiny specks of madness
Glinting in your eye

You wish to banish Tuesdays
You claim that trees can dance
You say that smiling's dangerous
And giraffes should all wear pants

You tried to smoke a carrot
Your bike has two square wheels
You wash your hair with Listerine
And you frequently kiss seals

People call you wacky
To others, you're a menace
To me you shall remain, forever
-Slightly different Dennis

Never the Whole Family

Rummaging through a box of old photographs
Images from the growing years
My days of greyscale memories
Snapped with stories attached

Images from the growing years
My sister, me and a kangaroo
Mum and Dad at Blackburn Lake

My days of greyscale memories
Seated on my father's lap
Mum holding my sister, the baby

Snapped with stories attached
Sub groups of a larger family
Never the complete set.

Fireflies

I saw fireflies once
In Prospect Park
Brooklyn

In the dying light around dusk
They suddenly appeared
Flitting, glowing

A magical first
Bright tiny dancers
Hovering in the gathering gloom

I saw fireflies once
Just once
In a park in Brooklyn

A light in my life
Forever shining
A memory well lit.

Mad Hairy Hands

I once told a kid called Clifford Cluff
-There are two signs you are going crazy
Really? asked Clifford
Yes, really
One sign is hairs growing in the palm of your hand

So, Clifford Cluff began peering closely at his hand
Searching for hairy signs of madness

What's the second sign?
Clifford Cluff asked

Looking for them...

I left Clifford standing there
-I just walked away-
Grinning all over my face.

Write It Down

Write it down
Write it down now
Before it gets a chance to escape
And never return
Before its light gets extinguished
-like a candle with the arrival of a sudden breeze
Write it down
Before all that's left of that fragile idea
Is a swirl of smoke
And not much else
Write it down
While it glows brightly
While it shines its special light
Write it down

Crafty Cushion Creatures

Let me warn you
Of those crafty cushion creatures
Lying in wait
For unsuspecting couch potatoes
Who sits mesmerized for hours
Staring at flashing television screens

Let me warn you
Of crafty cushion creatures
Who steal coins from pockets
And crumbs and biscuit morsels
Slips of papers, small toys
And the occasional lolly wrapper
Crumpled and folded flat

Let me warn you
Of crafty cushion creatures
Who collect lint and dust
Fine fragments of fluff
And the occasional earring
Secreting them
Within the dark recesses at the back of the couch
Beyond the view of those unsuspecting loungers

under Cover Agent

Pull back the curtains
Let in the light
Embrace the morning
Consign the night
Push back the covers
Roll out of bed
The day is awaiting
It has to be said

TICK-TICK-TICK
TOCK –TOCK- TOCK
Time is a wasting
So says the clock

Try that again...

Pull back the covers
Let in the light
Embrace the morning

Yeah okay...

Seeking Out Silence

A young man stood alone
On Frankston station
Like Warren Zevon
In splendid isolation

Into the heartland
Away from the crowd
Seeking out silence
The one thing that's loud

No conversation
No kick to kick
No singing duets
Life's a one ended stick

No rides on a see saw
No conversation
No playing chasey
Just splendid isolation

The Family Gathering

The family sit,
Surrounding the large wooden table of
gnarled oak

Throughout the day
They wandered through different landscapes
Thoughts dancing differently
Their eyes set upon separate scenes

But now
They meet at the intersection of family and dinner time
The deeds of the day entwine right here

Their voices float across the table
Conversation wraps around each of them
Rising and falling
Back and forth
Up and down the table

They dine together
Fine together
All around the table

And when every plate and spoon
knife and fork and napkin
Is cleared away
The goodbyes are shared
The hugs begin
And everyone wanders into the evening-
To their separate spaces

Yet fragments of the evening's conversation
Live again
In the minds of each of them
Together
Apart
Grateful for the gathering

winter wares on

The morning air
Sharp
Raw
Nips my face
And feasts on the breathe escaping from my mouth
Winter prowls in my garden
On my street, in the park
Its chilling presence
Waits at the corner
Ready to slap my face
With a blustery blast

I don my armour
Scarf
Gloves
Coat
-and sturdy boots
I am winter ready
Venturing into the cold zone
Squelching across the lawn
Trampling a mess of leaves
The clouds milling above me
Are mixing up an afternoon storm
A winter brew of hail and rain
I walk on, sinking into my coat
Defying the freeze
My winter wares on

Christmas Catastrophe

Our cat went mad the other night
And attacked our Christmas tree
All the bells and baubles
Were shattered in the spree
-And now she sits in contemplation
Amid the shattered decoration
Such a woeful sight to see
It's actually a catastrophe

Angel on the Tree

I saw her smiling down at me
The angel on our Christmas tree
She sits aloft with festive lights
I'm glad it's her -I'm scared of heights.

Stocking Time

I awoke on Christmas morning
And clambered down the stairs
I saw the Christmas stockings
Bulging with presents to spare
I noticed that my sister's
Looked slightly larger than mine
I considered swapping them over
-But I didn't cross that line.

Traffic Passing By

I saw you drive past
In the back seat of your family's car
Faced pressed to the window
And a look on your face
Like a blank piece of paper

You looked trapped
- A fish in a bowl perhaps?

I don't think you saw me
I was waiting at the bus stop
Sitting between a lady with purple hair
Who looked a bit like the Queen
And a kid wearing enormous headphones
Frying his brain with doof-doof music
Then the bus pulled up
And I got on board
Still wondering where you were going
In the backseat of your family's car.

Sunday Best was
How we Dressed

When I was still a little kid
Grown-ups fussed over how we dressed
When we stepped out, we were urged
To dress in what they called our Sunday best
Spit and polish
Tarted up
Dressed like it's the Melbourne Cup

Try to impress
Brush your hair
Polish your shoes
Show you care

It was like we were going to visit the Queen
Our outfits all so fresh and clean
Off to see rellies, movies, an outing
Always quiet
Never shouting

Sunday best
Was how we dressed

Science Rocks

The earth
And everything in it
Owes a debt
To Science

Every appliance
Is relying
On science

Every machine
That you've ever seen
Is dependent on science

My car
Wouldn't get far
Without science

Nature and trees
Sizzle and freeze
It's all science

Computer or phone
We're never alone
We've got science

As old as the earth
As moving as time
That's science.

Cat in the Window

Grandma's cat
Sir Fluffickins
Sits on the windowsill
Beside the floral curtains
Like a statue ever still

He stares at people
On the street
Slowly passing by
And no one seems to notice
His ever watchful eye

So the cat sits by the curtains
Curtains, faded by the sun
He stares
He purrs
And gazes out
Unseen by anyone

Losing Your Mind

Des lost his mind
So he climbed a tree
To find out
Where his mind might be

It wasn't that he used it much
But occasionally, he kept in touch

He looked in the garden
He stared at the sky
He scratched his head
But, he didn't know why

He then ate a pizza
He sat in a chair
He looked at his shoe
His mind wasn't there

At the end of the day
As darkness descended
Des stopped looking
All searching suspended

Somewhere far away
In a world free and wild
His mind roamed about
Like a freewheeling child

Des didn't mind
Des didn't care
He hadn't worried
When it was there

So, look after your mind
Don't neglect or abuse it
Or like poor old Des
You'll probably lose it

Nancy's Plan for Her Caravan

Mavis Davis's Nana, Nancy
Has a friend
Name of Clancy
His next door neighbour
Victor Vector
Is a caravan collector
Now Victor is a generous fellow
He lent Nancy a van -bright yellow
Now Nancy can explore the nation
On her long dreamed of vacation
Will she visit Ulladulla,
Birragurra, Turramurra?
Will she stop at Ararat, Ballarat
Winter's Flat?
Will she cruise through Parramatta, Wangaratta?
Does it matter?
Will she stay in Parabadoo?
Wooloomooloo, Cockatoo?
Tell me, would you?
Will she go to Boggabri, Woolamai, Narrabri?
Maybe she'll choose Bendigo?
Oh, I don't know
Go Nancy go!

An Attack of the Crankies

I'm in a cranky mood today
My happy's gone awry
I'm rather cross right now
I have a twitchy eye

I'm in a cranky mood today
With an awful attitude
My advice is steer clear
I'm sullen, grumpy, rude

I'm in a cranky mood right now
All I do is scowl
I'm a misery guts
If you come near, I'll growl

I'm in a cranky mood today
I could bite a crocodile
You should stay well away from me
I really am quite vile

I'm in a cranky mood today
They've sent me to my room
I'm pricklier than cactus
And wallowing in gloom

I'm in a cranky mood today
This poem has made me mad
I refuse to finish it
And I don't care if you're...

About the Author

Alan j. Wright has been writing, performing, and promoting poetry for most of his life. He has always loved words and the marvelous ways in which they can be used to paint pictures in the mind of the reader. Call him a logophile and he will smile...

This collection of adventurous and diverse verse for young poetry lovers builds upon Alan's previous books, 'Searching for Hen's Teeth' and 'I Bet There's No Broccoli on The Moon.'

Alan wishes it to be known that he loves tiramisu, once had a haircut in Mooloolaba, has visited Humpty Do, writes all his poems with his left hand and has never been skydiving.

'What the Poemster Found' is a collection of wide ranging poetry ideas gathered from those wondrous places poets like to roam in their never ending search for the word lightning to spark yet another idea.

Printed in the United States
By Bookmasters